NATIONAL
GEOGRAPHIC
School Publishing

W9-AYA-119

# States of Matter

**Mary Garcia**

**PICTURE CREDITS**
Cover, 4 (left), 7 (above), 8 (above), 9 (right), 10 (above), 12 (right), 14
(left), 15 (above), 17 (above), 19 (right), 20 (above and right), 15 (right)
Photolibrary.com; 1, 6, 7 (below), 11 (right), 12 (left), 18 (right) DK Images;
4 (right above), 5 (left above), 7 (right above), 10 (below), 13 (right), 17
(below), 18 (left), 20 (left) APL/Corbis; 4 (right below), 7 (right below), 8
(left), 21 (above) Alamy; 16 Guy Holt Illustration.

Produced through the worldwide resources of the National Geographic Society,
John M. Fahey, Jr., President and Chief Executive Officer; Gilbert M. Grosvenor,
Chairman of the Board; Nina D. Hoffman, Executive Vice President and
President, Books and Education Publishing Group.

**PREPARED BY NATIONAL GEOGRAPHIC SCHOOL PUBLISHING**
Steve Mico, Executive Vice President and Publisher, Children's Books and
Education Publishing Group; Marianne Hiland, Editor in Chief; Lynnette Brent,
Executive Editor; Michael Murphy and Barbara Wood, Senior Editors; Nicole
Rouse, Editor; Bea Jackson, Design Director; David Dumo, Art Director; Shanin
Glenn, Designer; Margaret Sidlosky, Illustrations Director; Matt Wascavage,
Manager of Publishing Services; Sean Philpotts, Production Manager.

**MANUFACTURING AND QUALITY MANAGEMENT**
Christopher A. Liedel, Chief Financial Officer; Phillip L. Schlosser, Vice
President; Clifton M. Brown III, Director.

**BOOK DEVELOPMENT**
Ibis for Kids Australia Pty Limited.

Published by the National Geographic Society
1145 17th Street, N.W.
Washington, D.C. 20036-4688

Product No. 4W1005060

ISBN-13: 978-1-4263-5056-6
ISBN-10: 1-4263-5056-2

2012 2013 2014 2015
1 2 3 4 5 6 7 8 9 10 11 12 13 14 15

Printed in the United States of America

# Contents

fizzy water

4

ice skaters

canoe

**Everything in the world is made of matter.**
**Talk about the things you see in these photos.**

goldfish bowl

paddle

river

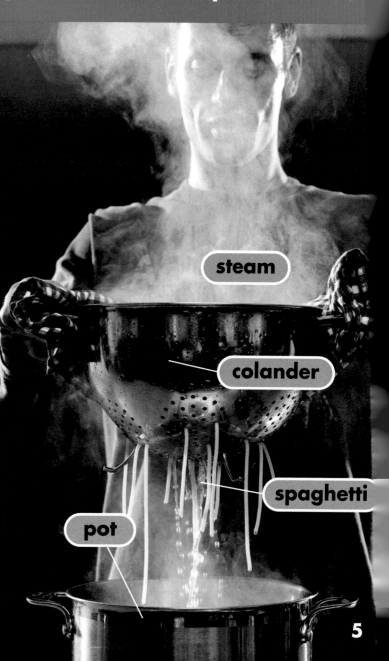

steam

colander

spaghetti

pot

# Talking About Matter

What is **matter**? Matter is anything that takes up space. The most common forms, or states, of matter are **solid**, **liquid**, and **gas**.

The air in this bubble is matter. The state of the air is gas.

These rocks are matter. The state of the rocks is solid.

This water is matter. The state of the water is liquid.

## Did You Know?

There is another state of matter called plasma. When you see streaks of lightning, you are seeing plasma. Plasma is also used in some TVs.

lightning

plasma TV

# Matter in Solid Form

If something is solid, it has its own shape.
If you move a solid from one place
to another, its size and shape stay the same.

This car travels from place to place.
It stays the same size and shape
because it is a solid.

This box can be moved. It stays the same size and shape because it is a solid.

Each of these marbles is a solid. The jar is a solid, too.

# Matter in Liquid Form

A liquid takes up space,
but it does not have a shape of its own.
Its shape depends on where it is.

The water in this stream
flows over and around rocks.
The rocks help to give the stream its shape.

The water in this bathtub
is shaped the way the tub is shaped.

This girl is pouring a drink into a glass.
When the liquid is in the glass, it is
the same shape as the glass.

11

# Matter in Gas Form

A gas takes up space,
but it does not have a shape of its own.
Air is a gas.

The air inside a balloon is a gas. The air spreads out and fills the balloon.

This diver can breathe underwater using air from a tank.

The bubbles in soda are gas.

# From One State to Another

Matter can **change** from one state to another state. **Temperature** can change the state of matter.

The water in this river froze. The water changed to solid **ice**.

**Heat** makes the solid wax of a candle **melt**.
The solid wax becomes liquid wax.
When the wax cools, it becomes solid again.

The water in this kettle boils.
The heat changes the water to **steam**.

Water can change from one state to another state. This is happening in nature all the time.

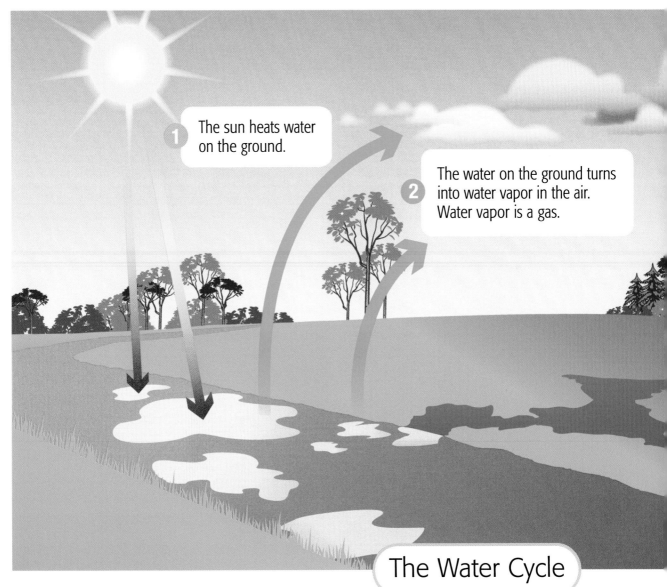

The sun heats water on the ground.

The water on the ground turns into water vapor in the air. Water vapor is a gas.

The Water Cycle

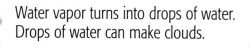

Water vapor turns into drops of water. Drops of water can make clouds.

Water on the ground turns into water vapor in the air.

④ Water in the clouds falls back to Earth as rain.

Water in the clouds falls back to Earth as rain.

Sometimes when we change the state of matter, we can't change it back to its first state.

This concrete is liquid when it is poured.
The liquid hardens into a solid.
The concrete cannot become a liquid again.

This pancake mixture is a liquid.
The mixture is cooked and becomes solid pancakes.
The pancakes cannot become liquid again.

Glass is made from a special sand.
The sand melts into a liquid when
it is heated. This glassblower
is making a glass object.

ice cream cone

river

orange juice

20

# Talk about these pictures.
## What do they show about the different states of matter?

tea kettle

water slide

change

gas

heat

ice

liquid

matter

melt

solid

steam

temperature

# Glossary

**change** (page 14)
To make something different
Matter can change from one state to another state.

**gas** (page 6)
A state of matter that doesn't have a definite size or shape
You can't always see a gas.

**heat** (page 15)
To make something hot
When you heat wax, it melts.

**ice** (page 14)
Frozen water
When you freeze water, it becomes ice.

**liquid** (page 6)
A state of matter that takes up space but does not have a definite shape
A liquid changes shape to fit the space it is in.

**matter** (page 6)
Anything that takes up space
Everything in the world is made of matter.

**melt** (page 15)
To make something liquid by heating it
Ice cream will melt in the sun.

**solid** (page 6)
A state of matter that has a definite shape and size
A solid does not change size or shape.

**steam** (page 15)
The vapor that comes from water when it is heated
Steam rises from water when water is boiled.

**temperature** (page 14)
The measure of how hot or cold something is
Temperature can make matter change from one state to another state.

# Index